Peaceful
Coloring
Book

Peaceful Coloring Book

THUNDER BAY
P · R · E · S · S
San Diego, California

Thunder Bay Press

An imprint of Printers Row Publishing Group

10350 Barnes Canyon Road, Suite 100, San Diego, CA 92121

www.thunderbaybooks.com • mail@thunderbaybooks.com

Text and design © 2020 Arcturus Holdings Limited

Correspondence regarding the content of this book should be sent to Thunder Bay Press, Editorial Department, at the above address. Author and rights inquiries should be sent to Arcturus Holdings Limited, 26/27 Bickels Yard, 151-153 Bermondsey Street, London SE1 3HA, England; info@arcturuspublishing.com.

Thunder Bay Press

Publisher: Peter Norton • Associate Publisher: Ana Parker

Editor: Dan Mansfield

Acquisitions Editor: Kathryn Chipinka Dalby

ISBN: 978-1-64517-647-3

CH008578NT

Printed in Malaysia

24 23 22 21 20 1 2 3 4 5

Introduction

Switch off that smartphone for a while and switch on to a totally different way of spending your spare time, with the *Peaceful Coloring Book*. Empty your mind of background noise and simply chill, shading in images with a set of pens or pencils, and you will be amazed at the benefits it brings.

The calming predictability of coloring helps us to focus on the moment, increasing our creativity and sense of well-being. The outlines in these pages include imaginative patterns and mandalas, together with line drawings of animals, flowers, and even fungi! Welcome to a world of coloring fun, all in a handy format.

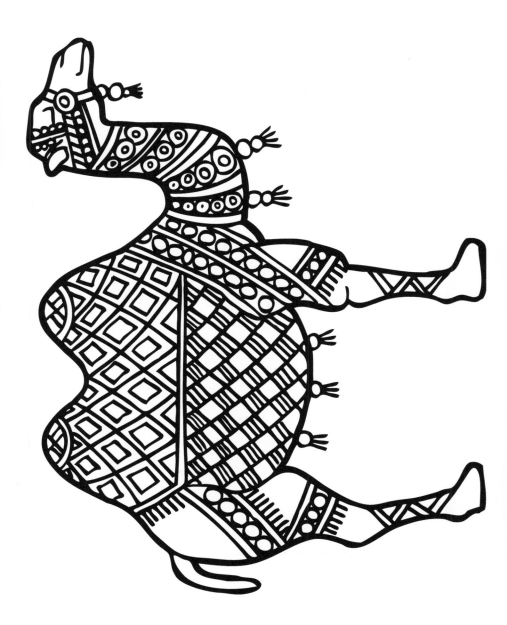

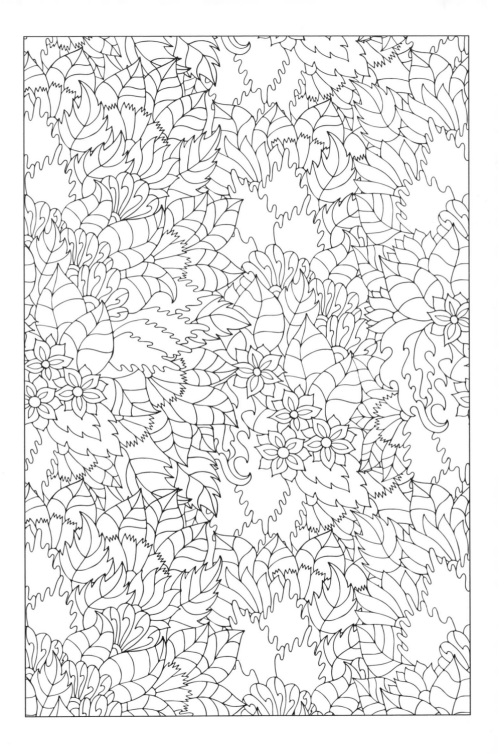

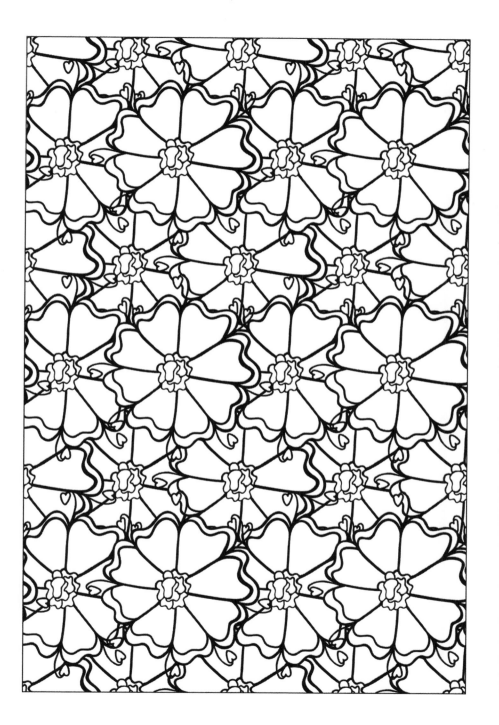

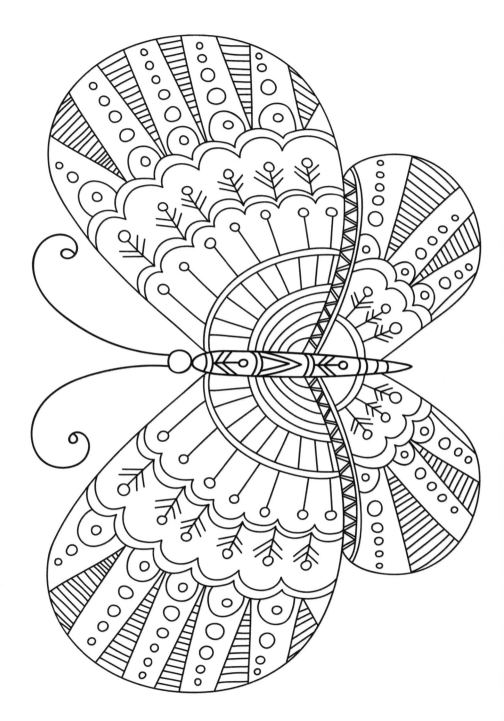